Painting on
Pottery

First published in Great Britain in 2019 by

Search Press Limited
Wellwood
North Farm Road
Tunbridge Wells
Kent TN2 3DR

© 2018, Éditions Marie Claire-Société d'Information et de Créations (SIC)

Original French title: *La Peinture Sur Porcelaine pas à pas*

English translation by Burravoe Translation Services

ISBN: 978-1-78221-760-2

PICTURE CREDITS
Shutterstock: ©Sergey Nivens; ©Geo-grafika; ©Graphicaffe; ©nubenamo; ©Olga Skorobogatova (pp. 52,84); ©Julialopez (pp. 32, 33, 74, 75); ©Alenka Karabanova (pp. 46, 58, 78, 90, 94); ©Milan M; ©Fribus Mara

SUPPLIERS
PÉBÉO
www.pebeo.com

ACKNOWLEDGEMENTS
Thank you to
Maison de la porcelaine for all the wonderful items I have been able to use.

Thank you to Truffaut for allowing us to do a more than sufficient shop!

Thanks to Adeline and Flore for their trust and the freedom that they give me.

Thanks to Charlotte and Patrice for their talent and good humour.

Thanks to Isabelle for her rigorous approach and eagle eyes.

TANIA ZAOUI

Painting on
Pottery

22 modern, colourful designs

SEARCH PRESS

INTRODUCTION

If you love patterns or enjoy making handmade presents, but you're frustrated that you do not have access to pottery classes or a kiln for glazing your creations – this book is for you! A few pots of Pébéo Porcelaine 150 paint, some plain, shop-bought crockery and a domestic oven is all you need to achieve an infinite number of creative projects.

But first let's have a look at this magical paint and what it can be used on. All the projects in this book can be done on any ceramic material (a term covering a whole family of materials including terracotta, earthenware, stoneware and porcelain).

The word 'ceramic' actually comes from the Greek word 'keramos', meaning clay. Ceramic material differs according to the physical composition of the clay and the heat at which it is baked. There are two main families: porous clay (earthenware, terracotta and certain types of stoneware) and impermeable clay (porcelain and some stoneware), which fire at higher temperatures.

A good way to tell the difference between earthenware and porcelain is to hold the item up to the light – if you can see the light through it, it is porcelain; if not, it is earthenware.

We have used Pébéo Porcelaine 150 paints, which allow you to imitate professional glazes using a simple domestic oven. There are 46 colours in the range that are fixed by simply baking at 150°C. These include transparent, pastel and opaque colours, as well as shimmers. The colours can be mixed together. There are also marker pens for producing fine lines or writing. Once baked, the decorated items can even go through the dishwasher. It's time to give your crockery a makeover!

One final tip: do not stress about getting things wrong – it is one of the secrets of being creative. In my case, it is often by venturing off the beaten track in terms of tools and techniques that I discover new things and end up surprising myself! Do not judge yourself too harshly; better simply to move on to decorating the next plate and consider any abandoned projects a useful record of your progress.

So get out your brushes and let's get going!

CONTENTS

Basic Techniques   8

Colour chart _____ 8
Instructions _____ 9
Creating different effects _____ 10

For the Dining Table   12

Small Bowls _____ 14
Egg Cups _____ 18
Blue and Copper Plates _____ 22
Cup and Saucer _____ 23
Lucky Eye Coffee Set _____ 28

For the Living Room   32

Flowerpots _____ 34
Pen Pot and Change Tray _____ 38
Wall Decoration _____ 39
Vases _____ 44
Lamp _____ 48
Upcycled Vases _____ 49

For the Kitchen   54

Carafe and Goblet _____ 56
Kitchen Utensils Pot _____ 60
Small Coffee Jars _____ 61
Mosaic-effect Tiles _____ 66
Leopard Plate _____ 70

For the Bathroom   74

Japanese Flower Bowls _____ 76
Toothbrush Holder and Soap Dish _____ 77
China Earrings _____ 82
Blue and Gold Tray and Pot _____ 86
Necklace _____ 87
Ring Holder _____ 92

Tender pink 50

Mango 49

Marseilles yellow 02

Water green 53

Turquoise 20

Emerald 19

Lapis blue 16

Shimmer petroleum 109

Chalkboard black 201

Scarlet red 06

Vermeil gold 45

Colour chart

These are some of the most widely used colours in this book.

BASIC TECHNIQUES

Instructions

Before you do anything else, ensure the items you are going to paint are completely grease-free by cleaning them with alcohol or soapy water, then drying them carefully.

To dilute the colours, use the Pébéo Porcelaine 150 thinner. This gives you a more liquid colour without losing any intensity – very practical for large areas.

Make sure you shake the marker pens well before use. Then pump the tip up and down several times to get them ready for first use. Store them flat.

If your designs 'go wrong', soak them before cleaning off the paint with a sponge (reserve one especially for this purpose).

Wash paintbrushes in soapy water before use.

Give your projects time to dry: the surface will be touch-dry in a matter of minutes but it will be a minimum of 24 hours before it is dry right through.

The baking time for all colours and markers in the range is 35 minutes at 150°C (300°F, gas mark 2) in a domestic oven, but you must always leave a minimum of 24 hours' drying time beforehand.

After baking, it is fine to put the items you have painted through the dishwasher and use your usual washing-up liquid, alcohol, solvents and detergents on them. To ensure they stand the test of time, use an 'eco' machine cycle and put them in the top basket.

> **Safety note:** Pebeo paints are safe to use on cups, plates, etc. However, if you intend to use them for eating and drinking from on a daily basis, it is recommended that you paint only those surfaces that will not come into direct contact with food or drink.

Creating different effects

- - - - - - - - - -

Here is an overview of possible effects:
these samples were made using an Anthracite black marker and Pébéo paint in Lapis blue 16 and Abyss black 41.

1 Stencil and atomizer spray

• To use this paint in an atomizer spray, thin your colour, adding half the Porcelaine 150 thinner. This will prevent the nozzle from clogging.

• You can create your own stencil by cutting out shapes from self-adhesive plastic. You can also experiment with stickers and masking tape. Warning: do not spray the paint on too thickly; it may peel away with the stencil.

2 Scratched glaze

I discovered this technique by mistake. It gives an effect a bit like etching: I painted on a thin layer of Lapis blue paint with the thick brush and after leaving it to dry for ten minutes, I scratched the surface with the point of a scalpel.

Then I used the thick brush to paint on another thin layer of black, waited ten minutes, then used the scratching technique a final time.

I used the same technique under the black stripe with a single layer of black.

3 Marker pens

• Fine tip marker 0.7mm Anthracite black
• Bullet tip marker 1.2mm Anthracite black
Shake well before using, pump the tip up and down on a sheet of paper to get the ink flowing and store them flat.

As you can see, it is not always possible to get the ink to flow easily and at a steady pace, but this just adds to the effect.

4 Paintbrushes

After trying some lines using markers, it's time to move on to a paintbrush.

Have a go and get used to the feel.

5 Engraving

Lines are scratched with a scalpel on a thin wash of Lapis blue. Precise designs can be achieved by removing the paint, as in the Flowerpots and Leopard Plate (see pages 34 and 70).

6 Combining tools

I drew lines with a marker pen over a Lapis blue wash. This technique is used for the Pen Pot (see page 38).

For the Dining Table

Small Bowls

Dots, lines and crosses give these bowls an exotic feel - you can make as many as you like.

1

SMALL BOWLS

MATERIALS

- **Three bowls**
- **Pébéo Porcelaine 150 paint: Turquoise 20**
- **A Pébéo Porcelaine 150 marker, 1.2mm tip: Anthracite black**
- **A Pébéo Porcelaine 150 marker, 0.7mm tip: Anthracite black**
- **Paintbrushes: sizes 2 and 4**

Safety note: for bowls intended for regular food use, you are advised to avoid decorating the inner surfaces.

METHOD

Bowl 1

Draw two rows of crosses round the top of the bowl using the 0.7mm marker. Leave to dry.

Use the size 4 paintbrush to paint a Turquoise band below the crosses. Leave to dry.

Draw four parallel lines using the 0.7mm marker, then cross-hatch with vertical lines over the top. Leave to dry.

Draw three rows of diamonds underneath. Colour every other diamond in black with the marker. Leave to dry.

Finally, use the 0.7mm marker to draw two lines around the bottom of the bowl. Leave to dry.

Bowl 2

Paint two Turquoise bands with a size 2 paintbrush round the top of the bowl. Leave to dry.

Draw two rows of spots using the 1.2mm marker. Leave to dry.

Using the 0.7mm marker, draw a row of vertical lines 1cm (½in) high, and then immediately below, a row of vertical lines 2cm (¾in) high. Leave to dry.

Bowl 3

Using the 0.7mm marker, draw a row of vertical lines 1cm (½in) high around the top. Leave to dry.

Draw four horizontal lines right round the bowl with the 0.7mm marker. Leave to dry.

Divide the lower part into four sections with the 0.7mm marker:

- paint one Turquoise
- cross-hatch another closely with the marker
- draw diagonal lines across another with the marker
- in the final section draw vertical lines with the marker, then fill the gaps between them with oblique lines to make chevrons.

Leave the bowls to dry for 24 hours. Bake in the oven at 150°C (300°F, gas mark 2) for 35 minutes.

2

Egg Cups

Use different colours and patterns so everyone at the table has
their own personalized egg cup!

EGG CUPS

MATERIALS

- **Four egg cups with bases**

For egg cup 1:
- **Pébéo Porcelaine 150 paint: Mango 49, Ivory 43, Chalkboard black 201**
- **A very fine paintbrush, size 2**
- **A fine paintbrush, size 4**
- **A flat brush, size 16**

For egg cup 2:
- **Pébéo Porcelaine 150 paint: Gold 44, Water green 53, Chalkboard black 201**
- **A scalpel**
- **A very fine paintbrush, size 2**
- **A fine paintbrush, size 4**
- **A flat brush, size 16**

For egg cup 3:
- **Pébéo Porcelaine 150 paint: Gold 44, Water green 53, Chalkboard black 201**
- **A Pébéo Porcelaine 150 marker, 1.2mm tip: Anthracite black**
- **A very fine paintbrush, size 2**
- **A fine paintbrush, size 4**
- **A flat brush, approximately size 16**

For egg cup 4:
- **Pébéo Porcelaine 150 paint: Gold 44, Chalkboard black 201, Emerald 19 mixed with a little Ivory 43**
- **A very fine paintbrush, size 2**
- **A flat brush, size 16**

METHOD

Egg Cup ❶

Using the size 16 brush, paint a 1.5cm (⅝in) band of Mango, 0.5cm (¼in) from the top, and paint the whole base the same colour. Leave to dry.

Paint the area between the two bands Chalkboard black using the size 16 brush. Leave to dry.

Paint rows of Ivory spots using the size 4 brush over the whole of the black area. Leave to dry.

Using the size 2 brush, paint four lines in Chalkboard black around the top and bottom of the Mango bands. Leave to dry.

Egg Cup ❷

Using the size 16 brush, paint the whole of the outside of the egg cup in Chalkboard black. Leave to dry.

Using a scalpel, scratch off the paint over a 1.5cm (⅝in) band around the middle of the upper part of the egg cup.

Use the size 2 brush to paint a Water green line above the scratched band. Paint rows of Water green dashes over the whole of the base. Leave to dry.

Using the size 4 brush, paint lines of Gold dots around the top of the egg cup and a line of dots like a necklace around the waist. Leave to dry.

Egg Cup ❸

Paint a 3cm (1¼in) band round the top of the egg cup in Water green using the size 16 brush. Leave to dry.

Paint the area below, down to the top of the base of the egg cup, in Chalkboard black. Leave to dry.

Using an Anthracite black marker, draw criss-cross lines over the Water green section. Leave to dry.

Apply Chalkboard black brush strokes using the size 4 brush over the lines you have drawn in black marker. Leave to dry.

Paint Gold lines using the size 4 brush around the top edge of the egg cup and where the Water green meets the black. With the size 2 brush, paint another line around the bottom of the black and around the bottom edge. Leave to dry.

Egg Cup

Paint a 2cm (¾in) band round the top of the egg cup in Emerald using the size 16 brush. Leave to dry. You can scratch off any smudges with the scalpel.

Apply some Ivory criss-cross lines with the size 2 brush. Leave to dry.

Paint four Gold parallel lines with the size 2 brush. Leave to dry.

Paint a Chalkboard black border around the bottom edge of the egg cup and around the top rim using the size 2 brush.

Leave the egg cups to dry for 24 hours. Bake in the oven at 150°C (300°F, gas mark 2) for 35 minutes.

Blue and Copper Plates

A few stickers and an atomizer spray are all you need to achieve
a designer-look set of plates.

4

Cup and Saucer

This attractive speckled effect is created with a few simple brush strokes.

BLUE AND COPPER PLATES

3

MATERIALS

- Three white 20cm (8in) diameter earthenware plates
- Pébéo Porcelaine 150 paint: Abyss black 41, Vermeil gold 45, Ivory 43
- Thinner (Pébéo)
- Round stickers, 1 and 1.5cm (approximately ½ and ⅝in) in diameter
- An atomizer spray (found in many travel kits)
- 0.5cm (¼in) wide adhesive tape
- A large flat brush, size 18
- A small flat brush, around 0.5cm (¼in), size 6

Safety note: for plates intended for daily food use, you are advised to avoid decorating the eating surfaces.

METHOD

Plate

Fill half the small spray bottle with Abyss black paint and the other half with thinner. Mix well by shaking.

Spray the plate generously with Abyss black paint. Leave to dry, then quickly dip a paintbrush in the Vermeil gold paint and, holding it above the plate, tap the brush on to the handle of a larger brush to flick flecks of Vermeil gold onto the surface. Leave to dry, then use this technique again with the Ivory paint.

Paint the rim in Vermeil gold.

Plate

Apply the 1.5cm (⅝in) diameter stickers in staggered rows over half the surface of the plate, and some adhesive tape in a concentric circle just inside the rim.

Fill half the small atomizer spray with Abyss black paint and the other half with thinner.

Mix well by shaking. Spray the whole plate. Leave to dry before peeling off the stickers and the adhesive tape.

Paint in the border in Vermeil gold.

Plate

Apply the 1cm (½in) diameter stickers around half the edge of the plate and apply adhesive tape to create an arc, dividing the plate in two.

Fill half the small atomizer spray with Abyss black paint and the other half with thinner. Mix well by shaking.

Spray over the surface with the stickers. Leave to dry before peeling off the stickers and the adhesive tape.

Paint the white part in Vermeil gold using a large size 18 brush. Leave to dry, then apply a second coat.

Leave the plates to dry for 24 hours. Bake in the oven at 150°C (300°F, gas mark 2) for 35 minutes.

CUP AND SAUCER

4

MATERIALS

- An earthenware mug and dessert plate
- Pébéo Porcelaine 150 paint: Lapis blue 16, Mango 49, Marseilles yellow 02 mixed with Ivory 43, and for sky blue mix half Ivory 43 with a quarter of Lapis blue 16 and a quarter of Water green 53 (adjust as necessary)
- A flat brush, size 6
- A paintbrush, size 8
- A Pébéo Porcelaine 150 marker, 0.7mm tip: Anthracite black
- A Pébéo Porcelaine 150 marker, 1.2mm tip: Anthracite black

Safety note: for cups and plates intended for daily use, you are advised to avoid decorating the surfaces that will come into direct contact with food or drink.

METHOD

Cup

Dip the paintbrush in the Marseilles yellow, then tap it against the handle of the larger brush to flick flecks of paint onto the cup. Leave to dry before repeating the process on the other side. Leave to dry.

Repeat the process using Mango and Lapis blue paint. Leave to dry.

Paint a stripe of Marseilles yellow around the handle, then a stripe of sky blue. Paint around the rim in sky blue as well. Leave to dry.

Finally, using a 0.7mm marker, draw one fine and one more widely spaced cross-hatched section on the handle. Intensify the lines on the more widely spaced cross-hatching with the 1.2mm marker. Leave to dry.

Saucer

Use the same technique as for stage one of the mug: flick flecks of Marseilles yellow and sky blue paint. Leave to dry.

Paint the rim of the plate Mango with the flat brush. Leave to dry.

Draw three concentric circles parallel to the edge of the plate with the 0.7mm marker. Cross-hatch with perpendicular lines around approximately ½ of the circumference. Leave to dry.

Leave to dry for 24 hours. Bake in the oven at 150°C (300°F, gas mark 2) for 35 minutes.

5

Lucky Eye Coffee Set

Get an extra kick from your morning coffee with this
1950s-style eye motif!

5

LUCKY EYE COFFEE SET

MATERIALS

- **Two appetiser bowls**
- **Two ceramic spoons**
- **Pébéo Porcelaine 150 paint: Turquoise 20, Gold 44, Chalkboard black 201**
- **A Pébéo Porcelaine 150 marker, 0.7mm tip: Anthracite black**
- **Paintbrushes, sizes 2 and 4**
- **A flat brush, size 6**
- **A scalpel**

Safety note: for cups and spoons intended for daily use, you are advised to avoid decorating the surfaces that will come into direct contact with food and drink.

METHOD

Cup

Draw five circles with the Anthracite black marker, 1cm (½in) from the top edge.

Paint them Gold.

Using the size 6 brush and Chalkboard black paint, draw the outlines of the eyes. Leave to dry.

Scratch off some Black paint with the scalpel to define the eyelashes.

Using the Turquoise paint and the size 4 brush, draw the dots underneath the eyes. Leave to dry.

Cup **2**

Use the Anthracite black marker to draw five circles halfway up. Paint them Turquoise using the size 6 brush, then leave to dry.

Using the size 4 paintbrush, paint the almond shape of the eyes in Black. Leave to dry.

Paint around the eyes in Gold using the size 6 brush. Leave to dry.

Spoon **3**

Draw in the iris and pupil with the Anthracite black marker.

Paint the concave part of the spoon Chalkboard black. Leave to dry then scrape off some of the Black paint around the eye to define the eyelashes.

Using the Gold paint and the size 2 brush, paint dots around the rim of the black part. Leave to dry.

Paint Turquoise dots along the handle with the size 2 paintbrush. Leave to dry.

Spoon

Draw the iris and the pupil with the Anthracite black marker.

Paint the concave part of the spoon Chalkboard black. Leave to dry, then scrape off some of the Black paint around the eye to define the eyelashes.

Paint a thick line along the top of the handle in Gold.

1

4

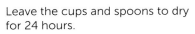

Leave the cups and spoons to dry for 24 hours.

Bake in the oven at 150°C (300°F, gas mark 2) for 35 minutes.

2

3

For the Living Room

6

Flowerpots

Simple terracotta pots take on a new and colourful look
with these graphic lines.

FLOWERPOTS

MATERIALS

- **Two small terracotta pots, 10cm (4in) in diameter, and one large pot, 14cm (5½in) in diameter**
- **Pébéo Porcelaine 150 paint: Turquoise 20, Chalkboard black 201, Tender pink 50, Mango 49, Marseilles yellow 02 mixed with Ivory 43**
- **Undercoat sealant**
- **A Pébéo Porcelaine 150 marker, 1.2mm tip: Anthracite black**
- **A Pébéo Porcelaine 150 marker, 0.7mm tip: Anthracite black**
- **Paintbrushes: sizes 2 and 4**
- **A flat brush, size 6**
- **A flat brush, size 10**

METHOD

All terracotta pots will need an initial layer of undercoat sealant. Allow to dry after application.

The large pot ❶

Using the 1.2mm Anthracite black marker and the Chalkboard black paint, draw lines to form crosses around the upper rim. Leave to dry.

Underneath, paint rows of Turquoise dots using a size 4 paintbrush. Leave to dry.

Paint a band of Turquoise dots 2.5cm (1in) high using the size 2 paintbrush.

Paint the rest of the pot Mango using the large brush. Leave to dry.

Using the 1.2mm marker draw rows of black dashes over a 2.5cm (1in) band. Leave to dry. Leave 2cm (¾in) unpainted.

Using the 0.7mm Anthracite black marker, draw two rows of crosses, then a final row with the 1.2mm marker. Leave to dry.

Paint the outside of the saucer in Turquoise.

The small pink and turquoise pot

Paint the upper rim in Tender pink using the size 6 brush. Leave to dry.

Draw vertical lines 3cm (1¼in) high underneath with the 1.2mm marker. Leave to dry.

Paint three rows of black spots using a size 6 brush overlapping the Tender pink rim and the black marker lines. Paint three more rows of black spots around the base of the pot. Leave to dry.

Paint a band of five rows of Turquoise spots around the middle using the size 4 paintbrush.

Leave to dry. Paint the inside of the saucer Chalkboard black and the outside in Turquoise.

The small yellow pot

Using the size 10 brush, paint four parallel lines in Marseilles yellow around the pot, leaving approximately 1.5cm (⅝in) between each one. Leave to dry.

Draw about seven vertical lines, spaced 3cm (1¼in) apart. Leave to dry.

Paint two rows of black dots with a size 4 paintbrush, overlapping the first yellow horizontal line. Repeat on the third yellow line. Leave to dry.

Do the same on the vertical between every other pair of yellow lines. Leave to dry.

Paint the inside of the saucer in Water green.

Leave the pots to dry for 24 hours. Bake in the oven at 150°C (300°F, gas mark 2) for 35 minutes.

Pen Pot and Change Tray

Brighten up your desk with these colourful accessories decorated
with fine cross-hatching.

Wall Decoration

This attractive wall hanging is quick and easy to make from a few fragments of
a china plate and some copper wire.

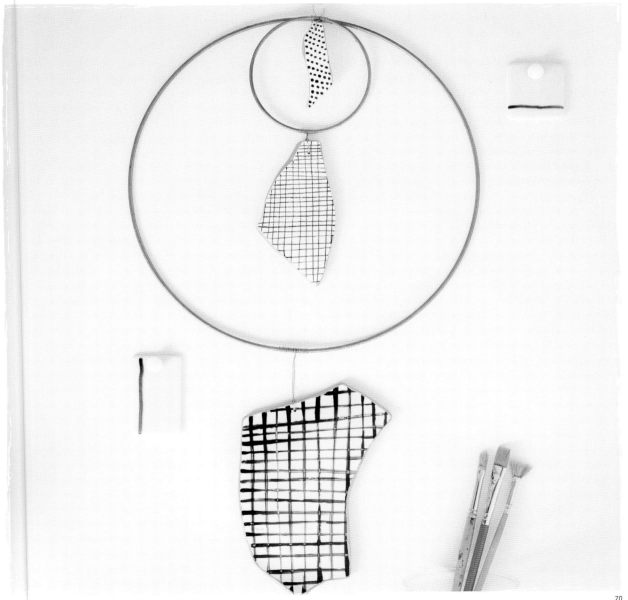

PEN POT AND CHANGE TRAY

MATERIALS

- A ceramic utensil holder
- A plain ceramic tray,
  13.5 x 12cm (5¼ x 4¾in)
- Pébéo Porcelaine 150 paint:
  Turquoise 20, Water green 53,
  Mango 49
- A Pébéo Porcelaine 150 marker,
  0.7mm tip: Anthracite black
- Flat brushes, sizes 18 and 10

METHOD

For the Pen Pot

Paint approximate circle shapes in each of the three colours, pushing the paint around with the brush.

Brush marks and transparent areas just add character. Leave to dry.

Draw vertical and horizontal lines with the marker to form a cross-hatched pattern over the top of, but slightly offset from, the coloured circles.

For the Change Tray

Use the same technique.

Leave to dry for 24 hours. Bake in the oven at 150°C (300°F, gas mark 2) for 35 minutes.

WALL DECORATION

8

MATERIALS

- **A second-hand 1950s-style earthenware plate**
- **Pébéo Porcelaine 150 paint: Abyss black 41 and Vermeil gold 45**
- **A Pébéo Porcelaine 150 marker, 0.7mm tip: Anthracite black**
- **Paintbrushes: sizes 2 and 4**
- **Copper wire**
- **Lamp shade rings, 8cm (3¹/₈in) and 23cm (9in) in diameter**
- **A hammer**
- **Sandpaper**
- **Mini-drill**

METHOD

Lay out a towel, put the plate on top of it, cover with another towel and tap with a hammer, gently at first. Keep checking on how the broken pieces are looking.

Sand the edges of one large piece, one medium-sized piece and one small piece of plate. Drill a hole through each of them with the smallest possible drill bit.

Paint the pieces in Vermeil gold. Leave to dry.

Using the size 4 brush, cross-hatch in Abyss black on the largest piece. Use the size 2 paintbrush to paint dots onto the smallest piece and use a marker to cross-hatch the medium-sized piece.

Leave to dry for 24 hours. Bake in the oven at 150°C (300°F, gas mark 2) for 35 minutes.

Take 30cm (12in) of copper wire and bend it in half. Use the bend as a loop to hang the decoration; place the wire at the top of the larger lamp shade ring, then wind each end round one side of the loop, attaching the smaller ring in place at the same time. Twist the ends together.

Slip 15cm (6in) of copper wire through the hole in the small piece of pottery and secure the other end by sliding it under the loop for hanging. Repeat the process for the other two pieces.

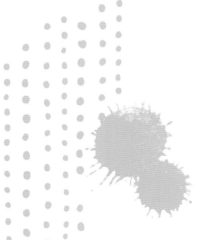

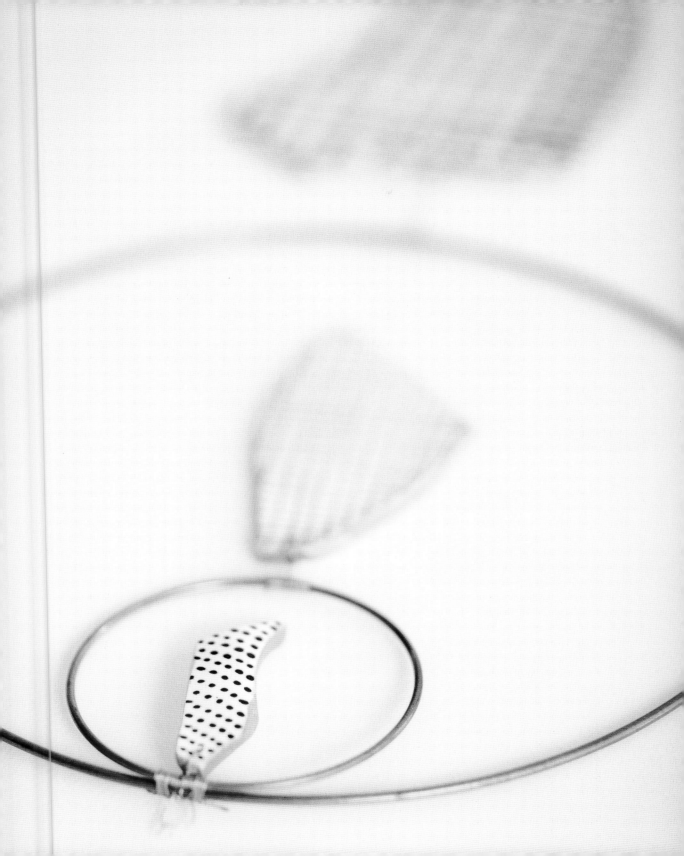

9

Vases

The black background beautifully highlights these
naive-style floral motifs.

9 VASES

MATERIALS

- A large oval vase
- A teardrop-shaped vase
- Pébéo Porcelaine 150 paint: Chalkboard black 201, Emerald 19, Lapis blue 16, Tender pink 50, Marseilles yellow 02, Turquoise 20
- A Pébéo Porcelaine 150 marker, 0.7mm tip: Anthracite black
- Paintbrushes: sizes 2 and 4
- A large flat DIY decorating brush
- Flat brushes, sizes 10 and 18
- A scalpel

METHOD

Use the Anthracite black marker to draw the flowers and leaves in a naive style, taking inspiration from the photograph.
Paint the leaves roughly in Emerald, the centres of the flowers in Marseilles yellow and the petals in Lapis blue, Tender pink or Turquoise.
Leave to dry. Paint round all the flowers and leaves in Chalkboard black. Leave to dry.
This is where the techniques for the two vases diverge.

Large Oval Vase

Add Chalkboard black paint haphazardly, leave to dry, then scratch off the inside of the flowers and petals using a scalpel. Go back over each section in its base colour to achieve a realistic engraved look.
You can add some pistils using the marker and the Chalkboard black paint.

Teardrop-shaped Vase

The scratching technique is not used here; instead draw all the details using the marker pen: cross-hatch the centres of the flowers and draw in the veins of the leaves and the stripes on the petals.

Leave the vases to dry for 24 hours. Bake in the oven at 150°C (300°F, gas mark 2) for 35 minutes.

10

Lamp

The charm of this lamp base lies in its irregular, handcrafted finish.

11

Upcycled Vases

Search out second-hand china to make these lovely characterful vases.

LAMP

MATERIALS

- **A square lamp base, 24 x 12cm (9½ x 4¾in)**
- **Pébéo Porcelaine 150 paint: Shimmer petroleum 109, Abyss black 41**
- **A large flat DIY decorating brush**
- **A scalpel**
- **Cable, switch and electrical fittings from an electrical supplier**
- **A lampshade**

METHOD

Roughly paint the lamp base, mixing Shimmer petroleum and Abyss black paint directly on the porcelain with your brush strokes. Leave to dry.

Scratch off vertical bands 1cm (½in) wide every 4cm (1½in), then do the same horizontally. An irregular finish is just what you are after.

Leave the lamp base to dry for 24 hours. Bake in the oven at 150°C (300°F, gas mark 2) for 35 minutes.

Attach the electrical fittings and the lampshade.

11

UPCYCLED VASES

MATERIALS

- **Two second-hand containers (we used a Limoges coffee pot and cup found in a second-hand shop)**
- **Pébéo Porcelaine 150 paint: Shimmer petroleum 109**
- **Stickers**
- **Narrow adhesive tape**
- **Flat brushes: sizes 10 and 18**

METHOD

Position the stickers over the flowers or patterns you want to retain. Stick adhesive tape over the gold border. This will prevent paint from spoiling it.
Use the large brush and the Petroleum paint to cover the whole surface area. Leave to dry.
Remove the adhesive tape and the stickers.

Leave the vases to dry for 24 hours. Bake in the oven at 150°C (300°F, gas mark 2) for 35 minutes.

For the Kitchen

12

Carafe and Goblet

The carafe and goblet have different designs but share black-based
colour schemes to give an ethnic look.

CARAFE AND GOBLET

MATERIALS

- **1 second-hand carafe**
- **1 second-hand goblet**
- **Pébéo Porcelaine 150 paint: Turquoise 20, Gold 44, Mango 49, Abyss black 41, Tender pink 50**
- **Paintbrushes: sizes 2 and 4**
- **Flat brushes: sizes 8 and 16**
- **A Pébéo Porcelaine 150 marker, 0.7mm tip: Anthracite black**

Safety note: for items intended for daily use, you are advised to avoid decorating the surfaces that will come into direct contact with liquids.

METHOD

Carafe

From top to bottom:

Paint the rim Turquoise using the size 2 brush, then apply a wider band of Gold with the size 4 brush. Leave 1cm (½in) white, then using the size 16 brush, paint a band 5cm (2in) wide in Mango.

Draw a line of triangles 3cm (1¼in) high with the marker pen, then paint the top triangles in Turquoise and the bottom triangles in Gold.

Add an Abyss black line with the size 4 brush. Paint a Mango band with the size 8 brush. Leave 2cm (¾in) white, then paint two Gold lines with the size 4 brush.

Use the brush to paint a 5cm (2in) band in Abyss black.

Paint the rest of the carafe Turquoise with the size 16 brush.

Goblet

From top to bottom:

Paint the rim Turquoise using the size 4 brush, then apply a band of Gold (still with the size 4 brush) and an Abyss black band approximately 2.5cm (1in) high with the size 8 brush.

Paint downward-pointing isosceles triangles, measuring 2.5cm (1in) along the base and 3cm (1¼in) along the sides (draw in first with the marker pen; the exact size will depend on the size of the goblet). Use the size 2 brush to paint along the edges and the size 4 brush to fill them in.

Paint the triangles formed underneath in Gold with the size 4 paintbrush.

Paint a band of Tender pink with the size 16 brush.

With the size 2 brush, paint a line of equilateral triangles measuring approximately 1.5cm (⅝in) along each side, then colour the upper row of triangles in Abyss black using the size 4 paintbrush and the lower ones in Gold.

Paint the neck of the goblet Abyss black, leaving a 1cm (½in) band at the bottom where you can alternate horizontal lines of Abyss black using the size 2 brush and Tender pink with the size 4 brush. Finish with a ring of Gold and a final band of Turquoise using the size 2 brush.

Leave to dry for 24 hours. Bake in the oven at 150°C (300°F, gas mark 2) for 35 minutes.

Kitchen Utensils Pot

This lovely practical pot can be made in a range of sizes to store
all your kitchen utensils.

Small Coffee Jars

These jars are ideal for taking your favourite coffee to work, and they're
on-trend with their irregular pattern of squares

13

KITCHEN UTENSILS POT

MATERIALS

- A large earthenware pot
- Pébéo Porcelaine 150 paint: Ivory 43, Lapis blue 16, Gold 44
- A large flat DIY decorating brush
- A flat brush, size 6
- A paintbrush: size 2

METHOD

Paint the outside of the jar Lapis blue using the large brush. Leave to dry.

Using the size 6 brush, paint five rows of dots in Gold round the top of the pot.

Using the size 2 brush, paint four rows of vertical dashes round the base of the pot in Ivory, leaving a plain blue section around the middle of the pot.

Leave to dry for 24 hours. Bake in the oven at 150°C (300°F, gas mark 2) for 35 minutes.

SMALL COFFEE JARS

14

MATERIALS

- **2 small china jars with lids**
- **Pébéo Porcelaine 150 paint: Lapis blue 16**
- **1 paintbrush: size 2**
- **1 flat brush, size 10**

> **Safety note:** for items intended for daily use, you are advised to avoid decorating the surfaces that will come into direct contact with food.

METHOD

Jar with large checks:
Using the flat brush, paint a thick grid pattern in Lapis blue, taking inspiration from the photo on page 61.

Jar with small checks:
Using the paintbrush, paint closely spaced cross-hatching in Lapis blue across the whole of the jar.

Leave to dry for 24 hours. Bake in the oven at 150°C (300°F, gas mark 2) for 35 minutes.

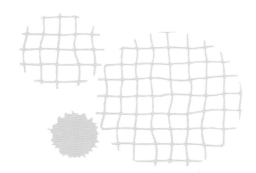

15

Mosaic-effect Tiles

These tiles are ideal as table mats or simply to add colour and
flair to your kitchen.

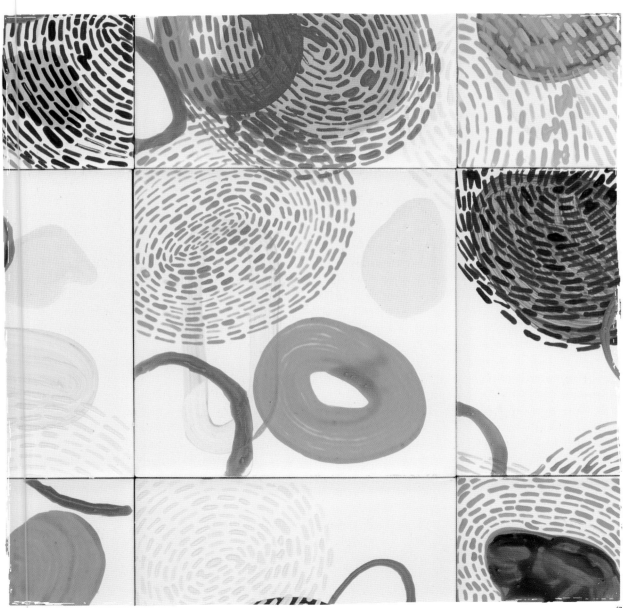

MOSAIC-EFFECT TILES

MATERIALS

- Square tiles, 10.5 x 10.5cm (4¼ x 4¼in) from DIY stores
- Pébéo Porcelaine 150 paint: Turquoise 20, Water green 53, Mango 49, Lapis blue 16, Tender pink 50, Emerald 19
- Paintbrushes: sizes 2 and 4
- A flat brush, size 8

METHOD

Place the tiles next to each other. Paint circular shapes and rings in various sizes and thicknesses, swapping between colours. Leave to dry.
Go round the circles and rings in concentric lines of dashes. Leave to dry.
Paint some Turquoise rings with the size 4 paintbrush which will give depth to the overall appearance.

Leave to dry for 24 hours. Bake in the oven at 150°C (300°F, gas mark 2) for 35 minutes.

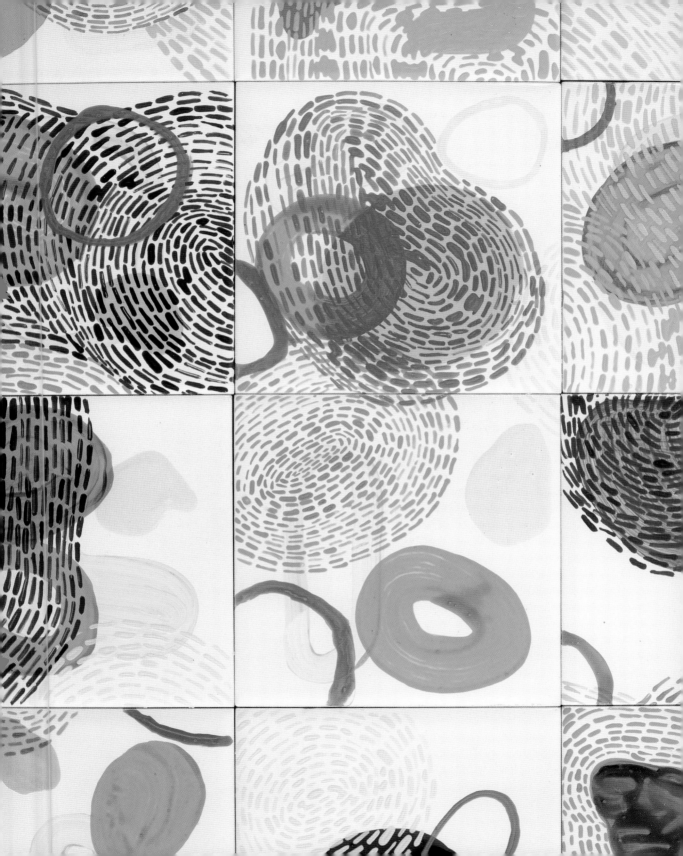

Leopard Plate

This stunning animal design is easy to achieve with a bit of imagination,
a paintbrush and a scalpel.

16

LEOPARD PLATE

MATERIALS

- An oval plate 33.5 x 21cm (13¼ x 8¼in)
- Pébéo Porcelaine 150 paint: Marseilles yellow 02, Emerald 19, Scarlet red 06, Chalkboard black 201
- A Pébéo Porcelaine 150 marker, 1.2mm tip: Anthracite black
- A Pébéo Porcelaine 150 marker, 0.7mm tip: Anthracite black
- A flat brush, size 6
- A paintbrush: size 8
- A scalpel

METHOD

Using the size 6 brush with the Chalkboard black, paint branches and twigs around the edges of the plate. Leave to dry.

Using the size 8 brush, paint the leaves in Emerald. Leave to dry. Apply touches of Scarlet red with the size 6 brush to create the flowers.

Leave to dry.

Draw the leopard with the 0.7mm marker, then colour it with Marseilles yellow.

Leave to dry.

Go over this with black dashes drawn with the 1.2mm marker. Leave to dry.

Use the scalpel to make the whites of the eyes stand out and scratch flecks of white into the yellow paint and black dashes.

Still using the scalpel, use the scratching technique to create the veins of the leaves, the shapes of the flowers from the red splodges and the texture of the branches.

Draw the leopard's face with the 0.7mm marker.

Leave to dry for 24 hours. Bake in the oven at 150°C (300°F, gas mark 2) for 35 minutes.

Safety note: for plates intended for daily food use, you are advised to avoid decorating the eating surfaces.

For the Bathroom

17

Japanese Flower Bowls

These bright and pastel-coloured bowls are great for storing jewellery,
makeup or sweets.

18

Toothbrush Holder and Soap Dish

*Give these bathroom essentials a modern makeover with just
a few strokes of the brush!*

17 JAPANESE FLOWER BOWLS

MATERIALS

- **Four flower-shaped teabag holders/appetiser bowls**
- **Pébéo Porcelaine 150 paint: Turquoise 20, Tender pink 50, Water green 53, Marseilles yellow 02, Ivory 43**
- **A Pébéo Porcelaine 150 marker, 1.2mm tip: Anthracite black**
- **A Pébéo Porcelaine 150 marker, 0.7mm tip: Anthracite black**
- **A flat brush, size 18**

METHOD

Paint each of the bowls a different colour: Tender pink, Turquoise, Water green and the last one a mixture of Marseilles yellow and Ivory, which will give a pastel yellow. Leave to dry.

Our bowls have raised patterns in the bottom; if yours have these, go over the raised parts with the markers. We used the 1.2mm marker for the centre and the 0.7mm marker for the petals. Alternatively, you can create your own patterns on a plain bowl.

Leave to dry for 24 hours. Bake in the oven at 150°C (300°F, gas mark 2) for 35 minutes.

Safety note: if your bowls are intended for daily food use, you are advised to avoid decorating the inner surfaces.

18

TOOTHBRUSH HOLDER
AND SOAP DISH

MATERIALS

- A plain soap dish
- A plain, square pen pot
- Pébéo Porcelaine 150 paint:
  Water green 53, Tender pink
  50, Shimmer petroleum 109,
  Emerald 19, Marseilles yellow
  02, Ivory 43
- A paintbrush: size 2

METHOD

Using the size 2 paintbrush, add dashes of all the colours in all different directions, making sure you leave plenty of undecorated space around them.

Leave to dry for 24 hours. Bake in the oven at 150°C (300°F, gas mark 2) for 35 minutes.

19

China earrings

You simply need to dig out an attractive piece of old china to create
these delicate earrings.

CHINA EARRINGS

MATERIALS

- A second-hand Limoges porcelain cup (or other old china)
- A pair of large hoop earrings
- Pébéo Porcelaine 150 paint: Scarlet red 06 and Tender pink 50
- Paintbrushes: sizes 2 and 4
- Copper wire
- Sandpaper
- An electric drill with a diamond-tipped drill bit
- Extra-strong transparent glue

METHOD

Gently break the porcelain cup. Select the two most similar fragments. Sand the edges.

Carefully drill a hole through the top at the centre of the fragment.

Mix the two paint colours together and use them to highlight and accentuate the patterns as you wish.

Knot the end of a 10cm (4in) length of wire through the drilled hole. Then pass it through the earring attachment.

Secure the knots with two dots of extra-strong glue.

Blue and Gold Tray and Pot

Irregular circles in shades of blue are beautifully offset with stripes of gold.

Necklace

Wear as a pendant to add a stylish touch to any outfit.

BLUE AND GOLD TRAY AND POT

MATERIALS

- **A rectangular tray, 16 x 12cm (6¼ x 4¾in)**
- **An earthenware pot**
- **Pébéo Porcelaine 150 paint: Lapis blue 16 and Gold 44**
- **Flat brushes, sizes 6 and 18**

METHOD

Paint staggered rows of Lapis blue spots over the whole of the tray and the pot by placing the tip of the size 6 brush on the surface and twisting it to create a circle. Leave to dry.

Tray:
Using the size 18 brush, paint one Gold stripe on the tray.

Pot:
Using the size 18 brush, paint three Gold vertical stripes on the pot.

Leave to dry for 24 hours. Bake in the oven at 150°C (300°F, gas mark 2) for 35 minutes.

21

NECKLACE

MATERIALS

- A second-hand 1950s-style earthenware plate
- Pébéo Porcelaine 150 paint: Vermeil gold 45
- Flat brush, size 10
- A gold or copper-coloured chain
- A lampshade ring, 8cm (3¼in) in diameter
- Copper wire
- Black thread
- Sandpaper
- An electric drill with a diamond-tipped drill bit

METHOD

Break the plate. Select a suitable fragment and sand the edges. Carefully drill a hole through the top at the centre of the fragment. Paint part of the fragment Vermeil gold with the brush.

Attach the ring to the chain and the china fragment to the ring using the copper wire.

Decorate the chain with two tassels, and attach two more at the top and bottom of the ring. To make the tassels, cut a dozen 5cm (2in) pieces of black thread, fold them in half round the point at which you want to position them, then twist copper wire around them to hold them in place.

Ring Holder

The oriental patterns give this ring holder plenty of personality.

22

RING HOLDER

MATERIALS

- **A plain ring holder**
- **Pébéo Porcelaine 150 paint: Chalkboard black 201, Turquoise 20 and Scarlet red 06**
- **A Pébéo Porcelaine 150 marker, 0.7mm tip: Anthracite black**
- **Paintbrushes: sizes 2 and 4**

METHOD

Use the size 2 brush to give the hand Scarlet red nails. Leave to dry.

With the size 4 brush, paint a bracelet around the wrist in the form of two rows of Turquoise spots.

Paint the tattoo design onto the fingers with the brush, and Chalkboard black, creating shapes like grains of rice. Paint a ring round the last three towards the base of the fingers (see photograph).

On the hand, draw the centre of a flower surrounded by petals with the marker pen.

Draw a scalloped circle around the flower, interspersed with grains of rice like the ones on the fingers. Draw two more scalloped circles. Use the marker pen to draw petals like fish scales around the scalloped circles until the whole of the back of the hand is covered.

Leave to dry for 24 hours. Bake in the oven at 150°C (300°F, gas mark 2) for 35 minutes.